M000012558

LAUGHS for LUNCH

BOB PHILLIPS

Illustrated by Norm Daniels

Evergreen
PRESS

Laughs for Lunch
by Bob Phillips
Copyright ©2006 Bob Phillips

All rights reserved. This book is protected under the copyright laws of the United States of America. This book may not be copied or reprinted for commercial gain or profit. Unless otherwise identified, Scripture quotations are from *The Living Bible,* copyright ©1971. Used by permission of Tyndale House Publishers, Inc., Wheaton, Illinois 60189. All rights reserved.

ISBN 1-58169-222-6
For Worldwide Distribution
Printed in the U.S.A.

Evergreen Press
P.O. Box 191540 • Mobile, AL 36619

Dedication

To Tyler, Owen, and Clayton...
who love to hear their
grandfather's jokes.

Introduction

A number of years ago a mother shared with me that she used to put little love notes on a napkin in her son's lunch. One day her son came home and said, "Mom, please do not do that any more. The kids who see the notes make fun of me, and it embarrasses me."

This creative mother changed her tactic. Instead of putting love notes on a napkin, she began to send him jokes from my books. He soon became very popular at school as he shared new jokes with his friends. Each day his friends would eagerly look forward to a new laugh for lunch.

Mom had the last laugh. She was still able to say I love you but in a unique and different way.

Laughs for Lunch contains enough pages to provide jokes for your youngster for half the school year (90 school days). The pages are perforated so all you have to do is tear out a page for each school day.

I hope your kids will have as much fun reading and sharing these jokes as I had putting them together. I've also added a Scripture passage for each day because man does not live on bread—or jokes—alone!

There's even a space to write a personal note, reminder, or greeting for the child you love so much. Have more than one child in school? Just buy enough copies of this book to go around! And for the second half of the school year, get *More Laughs for Lunch*.

Question: What nut sounds like a sneeze?
Answer: A cashew nut.

Question: If there is a red house on the right and a blue house on the left, where is the White House?
Answer: In Washington, D. C.

Tongue Twister
Repeat 3 times—out loud—as fast as you can:
Some shun sunshine on Sundays.

Question: What has a heart in its head?
Answer: Lettuce.

KNOCK, KNOCK.
Who's there?
Abbot.
Abbot who?
Abbot you don't know who this is!

Question: Where do hip geologists go to have a good time?
Answer: To rock festivals.

Lana: How do you fix a broken tomato?
Lark: You got me guessing.
Lana: With tomato paste.

How does a man become wise?
The first step is to trust and
reverence the Lord!
Proverbs 1:7

A Note for You! _____

_____

_____

_____

_____

_____

Question: What kind of saw lives in the sea?
Answer: A sea-saw.

Question: Why is it dangerous for farmers to plant peas during the war?
Answer: The enemy might come along and shell them.

Tongue Twister
Repeat 3 times—out loud—as fast as you can:
What a shame such a shapely sash should show shabby stitches.

Question: Why did the jelly roll?
Answer: Because it saw the apple turnover.

Question: What is a conversation among crazy dogs called?
Answer: A bowwow powwow.

Question: How does a kindergartner spell "farm"?
Answer: E-I-E-I-O

KNOCK, KNOCK.
Who's there?
Abe Lincoln.
Abe Lincoln who?
Hey pal! Don't you know
who Abe Lincoln is?

Question: How can you recognize rabbit stew?
Answer: It has hares in it.

Question: Which season do kangaroos like the best?
Answer: Springtime!

Only fools refuse to be taught.
Listen to your father and mother.
What you learn from them will stand
you in good stead; it will gain
you many honors.
Proverbs 1:8

A Note for You! _____

_____

_____

_____

_____

Question: What crazy shampoo do mountains use?
Answer: Head and Boulders.

Question: What do they call a collector of old magazines?
Answer: A doctor.

Tongue Twister

Repeat 3 times—out loud—as fast as you can:
Lean Lenny Long loves long Lenny lean.

Question: How do you make a slow employee fast?
Answer: Don't give him anything to eat for a while.

Question: What has leaves, but is not a plant?
Answer: A table.

KNOCK, KNOCK.
Who's there?
Ach.
Ach who?
God bless you.

Question: If you are invited out to dinner and upon sitting down you see nothing to eat but a beet, what would you say?
Answer: "That beets all!"

Luther: Where do moths dance?
Lydia: I'm in the dark.
Luther: At a mothball.

But all who
listen to me [Wisdom] *shall live*
in peace and safety, unafraid."
Proverbs 1:33

A Note for You! _____

_____

_____

_____

_____

Question: Where do crazy plants grow?"
Answer: In crackpots.

Question: Why shouldn't American girls learn Russian?
Answer: Because one tongue is enough for any girl.

Tongue Twister
Repeat 3 times—out loud—as fast as you can:
Luscious lemon liniment.

Question: What should you do to stop from getting sick the night before a trip?
Answer: Leave a day earlier.

Question: What animal has the highest level of intelligence?
Answer: A giraffe.

KNOCK, KNOCK.
Who's there?
A cheetah
A cheetah who?
A cheetah
never wins.

Question: How do you know when an elephant is in your bed?
Answer: By the E on his pajamas.

Leah: Where would you send a man to get an appetite?
Lawrence: I have no clue.
Leah: To Hungary.

---

*Every young man
who listens to me and obeys my instructions
will be given wisdom and good sense.*
Proverbs 2:1

A Note for You! _____

_____

_____

_____

_____

Question: What crazy cowboy steals teapots?
Answer: A kettle rustler.

Question: What should you do if you feel strongly about graffiti?
Answer: Sign a partition.

Tongue Twister
Repeat 3 times—out loud—as fast as you can:
Strange strategic statistics.

Question: What kind of dress do you have but never wear?
Answer: Your address.

Question: What has a mouth but no teeth?
Answer: A river.

KNOCK, KNOCK.

Who's there?

Adam

Adam who?

Adam up and get the total.

Question: What are 365 periods of happiness called?
Answer: A year.

Laurel: What does a frog order at a fast food restaurant?
LaVonne: I don't know.
Laurel: A burger and flies.

Yes, if you want better insight and discernment,
and are searching for them as you would for lost money
or hidden treasure, then wisdom will be given you and knowl-
edge of God himself; you will soon learn the importance of
reverence for the Lord and of trusting him.
Proverbs 2:3

A Note for You! _____

_____

_____

_____

_____

_____

Question: What do you get when you cross peanuts with golf balls?
Answer: Peanut putter.

Question: Why does the Statue of Liberty stand in New York Harbor?
Answer: Because it can't sit down.

Tongue Twister
Repeat 3 times—out loud—as fast as you can:
Six shy soldiers sold seven salted Salmons.

Question: When should you put a mouse in your sister's bed?
Answer: When you can't find a frog.

KNOCK, KNOCK.
Who's there?
Adelle.
Adelle who?
Adelle is what the farmer is in.

Question: What would you call a pig if it took an airplane ride?
Answer: Swine flu.

Lynette: Why was the woman only able to remember the names of people under five feet tall?
Leroy: I can't guess.
Lynette: Because she had a short memory.

For the Lord grants wisdom!
His every word is a treasure of knowledge
and understanding.
Proverbs 2:6

A Note for You! _____

_____

_____

_____

_____

_____

Question: Where do fish keep their life savings?
Answer: In a riverbank.

Question: If a soft answer turns away wrath, what does a hard answer do for you?
Answer: It turns wrath your way.

Tongue Twister
Repeat 3 times—out loud—as fast as you can:
Sly Sam sips Sally's soup

Question: What do you call something with a burning desire?
Answer: An arsonist.

KNOCK, KNOCK.
Who's there?
Divan.
Divan who?
Divan the pool and go swimming.

———

Question: What sort of offspring does a stupid florist have?
Answer: Blooming idiots.

———

Lila: What is the difference between a rooster, Uncle Sam, and a dance teacher?
Lillian: I have no idea.
Lila: The rooster says, "Cock-a-doodle-doo;" Uncle Sam says, "Yankee-doodle-doo;" and a dance teacher says, "Any dude'll do."

———

He grants good sense to the godly—his saints.
He is their shield, protecting them and
guarding their pathway.
Proverbs 2:7

A Note for You! _____

_____

_____

_____

_____

Question: If your aunt had rabbit ears, what would she be?
Answer: Antenna.

Question: What kind of waiter never accepts tips?
Answer: A dumb waiter.

Tongue Twister

Repeat 3 times—out loud—as fast as you can:
"Pucker, Pearl Potter, please," pleaded Pete Perkins politely.

Question: What gets lost every time you stand up?
Answer: Your lap.

KNOCK, KNOCK.
Who's there?
Adore.
Adore who?
Adore is between us. Please open up.

Question: How should you greet a German barber?
Answer: "Herr Dresser."

Lois: How many people does it take to clean up the hazardous waste dump?
Lola: You tell me.
Lois: Fifty. One tractor driver and 49 lawyers.

For wisdom and truth
will enter the very center of your being,
filling your life with joy.
Proverbs 2:10

A Note for You! _____

_____

_____

_____

_____

Question: What kind of car does Elsie the Cow drive?
Answer: A moo-ving van.

Question: What did the grape say when it was stepped on by an elephant?
Answer: Nothing...it just gave a little wine.

Tongue Twister
Repeat 3 times—out loud—as fast as you can:
Two tree toads tied together tried to trot to town twice.

Question: How do you define the daffodil?
Answer: A goofy pickle.

KNOCK, KNOCK.
Who's there?
Agatha.
Agatha who?
Agatha feeling you're fooling with me.

Question: Why would a complaint from a chicken be an insult?
Answer: Because it's a foul remark.

Luann: How did the father flea get home for Christmas?
Lowell: I give up.
Luann: By Greyhound.

Follow the steps of the godly instead,
and stay on the right path, for only good
men enjoy life to the full.
Proverbs 2:20-21

A Note for You! _____

_____

_____

_____

_____

_____

Question: How can you tell when a tree is truly frightened?
Answer: When it is petrified.

Question: What kind of sentence would you get if you broke the law of gravity?
Answer: A suspended one.

Tongue Twister

Repeat 3 times—out loud—as fast as you can:
The seething sea ceaseth seething.

Question: What is the difference between a mouse and a young lady?
Answer: One harms the cheese, and the other charms the he's.

KNOCK, KNOCK.
Who's there?
Ahead.
Ahead who?
Ahead is on your shoulders.

Question: Who invented the grandfather clock?
Answer: Pendulum Franklin.

Wendy: What is the difference between the rising sun and the setting sun?
Wesley: Who knows?
Wendy: All the difference in the world.

My son, never forget the things I've taught you.
If you want a long and satisfying life, closely
follow my instructions.
Proverbs 3:1

A Note for You! _____

_____

_____

_____

_____

Question: Why isn't your ear 12 inches long?
Answer: If it were, it would be a foot.

Tongue Twister

Repeat 3 times—out loud—as fast as you can:
Sweet Suzie Skunk sells sugar shakers.

Question: Why is an ex-boxer like a beehive?
Answer: An ex-boxer is an ex-pounder; an ex-pounder is a commentator; a commentator is an Irish tater; an Irish tater is a spectator; a spectator is a beholder; and a beholder is a beehive!

KNOCK, KNOCK.

Who's there?

A herd.

A heard who?

A herd you were home, so I came over!

Question: What did Snow White say when her pictures did not arrive back from the photo service?
Answer: Someday my prints will come.

Winthrop: How many nagging mothers does it take to screw in a light bulb?
Whitney: You've got me.
Winthrop: None. It's all right; I'll just sit here in the dark.

Never tire of loyalty and kindness. Hold these virtues tightly.
Write them deep within your heart.
Proverbs 3:3

A Note for You! _____

_____

_____

_____

_____

Question: Why did the frog sit on the lily pad?
Answer: Her sofa was being repaired.

Question: What do you do with a blue monster?
Answer: Cheer him up.

Tongue Twister

Repeat 3 times—out loud—as fast as you can:
Geese cackle, cows moo, crows caw, cocks crow.

Question: What does not break, no matter how far it falls?
Answer: A leaf.

KNOCK, KNOCK.

Who's there?

Aida.

Aida who?

Aida sandwich at lunch time.

Question: When is the best weather for gathering hay?
Answer: When it rains pitchforks.

Wilma: What is black and white and black and white?
Warren: My mind is a blank.
Wilma: A penguin tumbling down an iceberg.

If you want favor with both God and man,
and a reputation for good judgment and common sense,
then trust the Lord completely;
don't ever trust yourself.
Proverbs 3:4

A Note for You! _____

_____

_____

_____

_____

Question: What is an insane flower?
Answer: A crazy daisy.

Question: How long can a goose stand on one leg?
Answer: Try it and see.

Tongue Twister

Repeat 3 times—out loud—as fast as you can:
Beautiful babbling brooks bubble between blossoming banks.

Question: Why does a dog wag its tail?
Answer: Because it wants to.

KNOCK, KNOCK.
Who's there?
Akron.
Akron who?
Akron give you anything
but love, baby.

———

Question: What country makes you shiver with cold?
Answer: Chile.

———

Winifred: How intelligent is your pet duck?
Wilbur: That's a mystery.
Winifred: Very intelligent! I'll prove it by having him make a few wisequacks.

———

In everything you do, put God first,
and he will direct you and crown your efforts with success.
Proverbs 3:6

A Note for You! _____

_____

_____

_____

_____

Clarence: Write something on a piece of paper. Fold it, place it on the floor, and put your foot on it. I can tell you what is on the paper.
Carly: What is it?
Clarence: Your foot.

Question: What word is always pronounced wrong?
Answer: Wrong.

Tongue Twister

Repeat 3 times—out loud—as fast as you can:
Of all the saws I ever saw,
I never saw a saw that saws as this saw saws.

Question: How do you cheer a basketball player?
Answer: Hoop, hoop, hooray!

27

KNOCK, KNOCK.
Who's there?
Alaska.
Alaska who?
Alaska no questions. You tella no lies.

Question: Why does a little boy look one way and then the other way before crossing the street?
Answer: Because he can't look both ways at the same time.

Wimple: Who killed a fourth of all the people in the world?
William: I'm blank.
Wimple: Cain, when he killed Abel.

Don't be conceited, sure of your own wisdom.
Instead, trust and reverence the Lord,
and turn your back on evil; when you do that,
then you will be given renewed
health and vitality.
Proverbs 3:7

A Note for You! _____

_____

_____

_____

_____

_____

Question: Where do king crabs live?
Answer: In sand castles.

Question: When are hens not hens?
Answer: At night—when they become roosters.

Tongue Twister

Repeat 3 times—out loud—as fast as you can:
"Hark, an aardvark!" Mark barked for a lark.

Question: Why did the clown always handle money with his toes?
Answer: So it wouldn't slip through his fingers.

KNOCK, KNOCK.
Who's there?
Alby.
Alby who?
Alby glad when school's over.

Question: What fish is man's best friend?
Answer: The dogfish.

Willard: If a king sits on gold, who sits on silver?
Walter: I don't have the foggiest.
Willard: The Lone Ranger.

---

*Honor the Lord by giving
him the first part of all your income,
and he will fill your barns with wheat and barley and
overflow your wine vats with the finest wines.*
Proverbs 3:9

A Note for You! _____

_____

_____

_____

_____

Question: What do sharks eat with their peanut butter?
Answer: Jellyfish.

Question: What kind of seafood makes a good sandwich?
Answer: A jellyfish.

Tongue Twister
Repeat 3 times—out loud—as fast as you can:
Rush the washing, Russell!

Question: Why do we all go to bed?
Answer: Because the bed will not come to us.

31

KNOCK, KNOCK.
Who's there?
Alfred.
Alfred who?
Alfred the needle if you'll sew the button on.

Question: What increases in value by half when you turn it upside down?
Answer: The number 6.

Wanda: There is a donkey on one side of the deep river, and a bundle of hay on the other side. How can the donkey get to the hay? There is no bridge, and he cannot swim. Do you give up?
Wilson: Yes, I give up.
Wanda: So did the *other* donkey.

Young man, do not resent it when God chastens and corrects you, for his punishment is proof of his love. Just as a father punishes a son he delights in to make him better,
so the Lord corrects you.
Proverbs 3:11

A Note for You! _____

_____

_____

_____

_____

_____

*any similarity to this leg and the actual leg of Bob Phillips is purely coincidental!

Nurse: There is a man outside with a wooden leg named Smith.

Doctor: What is the name of his other leg?

Question: Which is faster: hot or cold?

Answer: Hot is faster. You can catch a cold.

Tongue Twister

Repeat 3 times—out loud—as fast as you can:
Four flat-backed fat blackbirds flew fitfully.

Question: What can you make by putting two banana peels together?

Answer: A pair of slippers.

KNOCK, KNOCK.
Who's there?
Ali.
Ali who?
Ali Bama is where I live.

Question: What pen is never used for writing?
Answer: A pigpen.

Walrus: How many doctors does it take to examine an elephant?
Willis: It's unknown to me.
Walrus: It depends on whether or not the elephant has health insurance.

---

*The man who knows right from wrong and has good judgment
and common sense is happier than the
man who is immensely rich!*
Proverbs 3:13

A Note for You! _____

_____

_____

_____

_____

Question: Why wouldn't the lightning bolt go to the storm?
Answer: Because it was on strike.

Question: What cord is full of knots that no one can untie?
Answer: A cord of wood.

Tongue Twister

Repeat 3 times—out loud—as fast as you can:
Pop dropped the slop mop when the cop stopped to hop.

Question: What do they call someone whose opinion differs from their own?
Answer: A radical.

KNOCK, KNOCK.
Who's there?
Alison.
Alison who?
Alison to the radio.

Question: Why is a kiss like gossip?
Answer: Because it goes from mouth to mouth.

Mother: For dessert, you have a choice of good or evil.
Son: What you mean?
Mother: Angel food cake or devil's food cake.

Wisdom is a tree
of life to those who eat her fruit;
happy is the man who keeps on eating it.
Proverbs 3:18

A Note for You! _____

_____

_____

_____

_____

_____

Question: What has four wheels, two horns, gives milk, and eats grass?
Answer: A cow on a skateboard.

Tongue Twister

Repeat 3 times—out loud—as fast as you can:
Sleep, sleep, sleep, the slim shepherd shouted sadly six times.

Question: What did Columbus stand on when he discovered America?
Answer: His feet.

KNOCK, KNOCK.
Who's there?
A little boy who can't
reach the doorbell.

Question: What do they call cabs lined up at the Dallas airport?
Answer: The yellow roll of taxis.

Son: They call a man's wife his better half, don't they?
Father: Yes, they do.
Son: Then I guess if a man marries twice, there's nothing left of him!

---

*Have two goals: wisdom—that is, knowing and doing right—
and common sense. Don't let them slip away, for they
fill you with living energy and bring
you honor and respect.*
Proverbs 3:21-22

A Note for You! _____

_____

_____

_____

_____

Question: What do short fairy-tale characters wear to look taller?
Answer: Rumple stilts.

Tongue Twister

Repeat 3 times—out loud—as fast as you can:
Silver thimbles.

Question: What has four legs but only one foot?
Answer: A bed.

KNOCK, KNOCK.
Who's there?
Allmen.
Allmen who?
Allmen act silly.

Question: In what month do girls talk the least?
Answer: February—because it's the shortest.

Question: What day of the year is a command to go forward?
Answer: March fourth.

Question: How do you spell mouse trap with three letters?
Answer: C-A-T.

Don't plot against your neighbor;
he is trusting you.
Proverbs 3:29

A Note for You! _____

_____

_____

_____

_____

_____

Have you ever seen a board walk? Have you ever seen a home run? Have you ever seen a hot dog stand? Have you ever seen a picket fence? Have you ever seen a salad bowl? Have you seen a shoe box?

Question: What lives in the forest, puts out fires, and has eight arms?
Answer: Smokey the Octopus.

Tongue Twister

Repeat 3 times—out loud—as fast as you can:
Shipshape suit shops ship shapely suits.

Question: What would a home be without children?
Answer: Quiet.

KNOCK, KNOCK.
Who's there?
Allotta.
Allotta who?
Allotta noise
you're making.

Question: Which is correct: the yoke of the egg IS white? Or the yolks of eggs ARE white?
Answer: Neither, the yolk of an egg is yellow.

Son: I'm really glad you named me Larry.
Mother: Why?
Son: That's what all the kids at school call me.

---

*Don't get into
needless fights.*
Proverbs 3:30

A Note for You! _____

.

_____

_____

_____

_____

_____

Question: What do you expect to be when you get out of school?
Answer: An old man.

Question: What question is never answered by saying "yes"?
Answer: Are you asleep?

Tongue Twister
Repeat 3 times—out loud—as fast as you can:
Round and round the rugged rock the ragged rascal ran.

Question: How can a leopard change his spots?
Answer: By moving.

KNOCK, KNOCK.
Who's there?
Althea.
Althea who?
Althea in my dreams.

Question: How do sailors identify Long Island?
Answer: By the Sound.

Passenger: Does this airplane fly faster than sound?
Flight attendant: It certainly does.
Passenger: Then would you please ask the pilot to slow down? My friend and I would like to talk.

Don't envy violent men. Don't copy their ways.
For such men are an abomination to the Lord,
but he gives his friendship to the godly.
Proverbs 3:31-32

A Note for You! _____

_____

_____

_____

_____

_____

Question: When the clock strikes 13, what time is it?
Answer: Time to get the clock fixed.

———

Question: Which is heavier, a half moon or a full moon?
Answer: A half moon, because the full moon is lighter.

———

Tongue Twister
Repeat 3 times—out loud—as fast as you can:
A shy little she said "Shoo!" to a fly and a flea in a flue.

KNOCK, KNOCK.
Who's there?
Amos.
Amos who?
A mosquito bit me.

Question: What kind of lights did Noah I have on his Ark?
Answer: Floodlights.

Daughter: Why is father singing so much tonight?
Mother: He's trying to sing the baby to sleep before the babysitter gets here.
Daughter: You know, if I were the baby, I'd pretend I was asleep.

Cling to wisdom—she will protect you.
Love her—she will guard you.
Proverbs 4:6

A Note for You! _____

_____

_____

_____

_____

Question: What happened when the musician died?
Answer: He decomposed.

Question: What's round and very, very, dangerous?
Answer: A vicious circle.

Tongue Twister
Repeat 3 times—out loud—as fast as you can:
Put pink paint and painted pots.

Question: What is the surest way to keep water from coming into your house?
Answer: Don't pay the water bill.

KNOCK, KNOCK.
Who's there?
Andy.
Andy who?
Andy mosquito bit me again.

Question: What would you get if you dropped chocolate on the beach?
Answer: Sandy candy.

Gertrude: What does the lighthouse keeper play in the Village Orchestra?
Gerhard: I can't guess.
Gertrude: The foghorn.

Getting wisdom is the most important thing you can do!
And with your wisdom, develop common sense
and good judgment.
Proverbs 4:7

A Note for You! _____

_____

_____

_____

_____

Question: What is a post office.
Answer: U.S. Snail.

Question: What do you call a gold digger?
Answer: A human gimmee pig.

Tongue Twister

Repeat 3 times—out loud—as fast as you can:
Maybe baby bees bounce in baby buggy buggies.

Question: What is a bore?
Answer: A person who can change the topic of conversation faster than you can change it back to yours.

KNOCK, KNOCK.

Who's there?
Andrew.
Andrew who?
Andrew a picture of me today
and it looked silly.

———

Question: What is another name for income tax?
Answer: Capital punishment.

———

Gustave: What do you serve when an oat comes to dinner?
Gilberta: I have no idea.
Gustave: Oatmeal.

———

If you exalt wisdom, she will exalt you.
Hold her fast, and she will lead you to great honor;
she will place a beautiful crown upon your head.
Proverbs 4:8

A Note for You! _____
_____
_____
_____
_____

Question: What did Mrs. Bullet say to Mr. Bullet?
Answer: Darling, I'm going to have a BB.

Tongue Twister

Repeat 3 times—out loud—as fast as you can:
Soldiers' shoulders shudder when shrill shells shriek.

Question: What do they call six women with one luncheon check?
Answer: Chaos.

Question: Why do the birds fly south for the winter?
Answer: Because it's too far to walk.

KNOCK, KNOCK.

Who's there?
Anita.
Anita who?
Anita minute to
think it over.

Question: How do you catch an electric eel?
Answer: With a lightning rod.

Geneva: What is the oldest form of social security?
Guthrie: You tell me.
Geneva: Suspenders.

I would have you learn this great fact:
that a life of doing right is the wisest life there is.
Proverbs 4:11

A Note for You! _____

_____

_____

_____

_____

Question: What did the 300 pound mouse say?
Answer: Here kitty, kitty, kitty.

Question: What do they call a boxer who gets beat up in a fight?
Answer: A sore loser.

Tongue Twister

Repeat 3 times—out loud—as fast as you can:
A critical cricket critic.

KNOCK, KNOCK.

Who's there?
Annette.
Annette who?
Annette is needed to
catch butterflies.

———

Question: What falls often but never gets hurt?
Answer: Rain.

———

Grover: Why should people never suffer from hunger in the Sahara Desert?
Gretchen: I give up.
Grover: Because of the sand which is there.

———

Carry out my instructions; don't forget them,
for they will lead you to real living.
Proverbs 4:13

A Note for You! _____

_____

_____

_____

_____

Question: Why does an elephant wear sunglasses?
Answer: If you were the one they were telling all these jokes about, you would want to hide too.

Question: Why does a fireman wear red suspenders?
Answer: To hold up his pants.

Tongue Twister
Repeat 3 times—out loud—as fast as you can:
Who'll wet the whetstone while Willie whistles wistfully?

Question: What is another name for a nightclub?
Answer: A rolling pin.

KNOCK, KNOCK.
Who's there?
Annie.
Annie who?
Annie-body seen my lost dog?

———

Question: How do you make a Big Mac® monster burger?
Answer: You put two people patties, special sauce, lettuce, cheese, pickles, and onions on a sesame seed bun.

———

Gwendolyn: If two is company and three is a crowd, what are four and five?
Godfrey: Who knows?
Gwendolyn: Nine.

———

Listen, son of mine, to what I say. Listen carefully.
Keep these thoughts ever in mind; let them penetrate
deep within your heart, for they will mean
real life for you and radiant health.
Proverbs 4:20-22

A Note for You! _____

_____

_____

_____

_____

_____

Question: What is it that even the smartest person will over-look?
Answer: His nose.

———

Question: What is another name for coffee?
Answer: Break fluid.

———

Tongue Twister

Repeat 3 times—out loud—as fast as you can:
Six shining soldiers.

KNOCK, KNOCK.
Who's there?
Apollo.
Apollo who?
Apollo you anywhere if you treat me nice!

Question: How should you refer to a tailor when you don't remember his name?
Answer: Mr. So-and-so.

Gideon: How do you divide 19 apples equally among 13 boys if eight of the apples are small?
Gloria: You've got me.
Gideon: By making applesauce.

Above all else, guard your affections.
For they influence everything else in your life.
Proverbs 4:23

A Note for You! _____

_____

_____

_____

_____

Question: Where can you always find happiness?
Answer: In the dictionary.

Question: When is it proper to refer to a person as a pig?
Answer: When he is a bore.

Tongue Twister
Repeat 3 times—out loud—as fast as you can:
Dick Hickey snickered niggardly, sticky bricks.

Question: What was the largest island before Australia was discovered?
Answer: Australia.

KNOCK, KNOCK.
Who's there?
Apricot.
Apricot who?
Apricot my key. Please open up!

Question: What is always behind time?
Answer: The back of a watch.

Question: What is the best day to fry food?
Answer: Friday.

Take a lesson from the ants, you lazy fellow.
Learn from their ways and be wise!
For though they have no king to make them work,
yet they labor hard all summer, gathering
food for the winter.
Proverbs 6:6-8

A Note for You! _____

_____

_____

_____

_____

Question: If you reached into your pants pocket and pulled out a $10 bill from each pocket, what would you have?
Answer: Somebody else's pants on.

Question: How many balls of string would it take to reach the moon?
Answer: Only one if it was long enough.

Tongue Twister
Repeat 3 times—out loud—as fast as you can:
Which wristwatches are Swiss wristwatches?

KNOCK, KNOCK.
Who's there?
Archer.
Archer who?
Archer mother and
father at home?

Question: Which day is stronger: Sunday or Monday?
Answer: Sunday is stronger. Monday is a weekday.

Question: Which is the largest room in the world?
Answer: The room for improvement.

For there are six things the Lord hates—no, seven:
haughtiness, lying, murdering, plotting evil, eagerness
to do wrong, a false witness, sowing
discord among brothers.
Proverbs 6:16

A Note for You! _____

_____

_____

_____

_____

_____

Question: What do you say to a hitchhiking frog?
Answer: Hop in!

Question: What did the nearsighted gingerbread boy use for eyes?
Answer: Contact raisins.

Tongue Twister
Repeat 3 times—out loud—as fast as you can
Sister Suzie's sewing shirts for soldiers.

KNOCK, KNOCK.
Who's there?
Arthur.
Arthur who?
Arthur mometer
is broken.

———

Question: Where do Eskimos keep their money?
Answer: In a snowbank.

———

Curtis: Why don't astronauts get hungry in outer space?
Cassandra: I don't know. Why?
Curtis: Because they just had a big launch.

———

Young man, obey your father and your mother.
Take to heart all of their advice; keep in
mind everything they tell you.
Proverbs 6:20-21

A Note for You! _____

_____

_____

_____

_____

Question: What do you call a knot that never remembers?
Answer: A forget-me-not.

Question: What's green and goes slam, slam, slam, slam?
Answer: A four-door pickle.

Tongue Twister

Repeat 3 times—out loud—as fast as you can
The girth of the earth giveth birth to mirth.

Question: What do you do if you have cobwebs in your brain?
Answer: Use a vacuum cleaner.

KNOCK, KNOCK.
Who's there?
Aster.
Aster who?
Aster yourself.

Question: How many sides does a circle have?
Answer: Two. Inside and outside.

Clem: What should you buy if you want to carry milk around on your wrists?
Carmen: I don't know.
Clem: A quartz watch.

Obey me and live!
Guard my words as your most precious possession.
Write them down, and also keep them
deep within your heart.
Proverbs 7:2-3

A Note for You! _____

_____

_____

_____

_____

Question: Why are oysters lazy?
Answer: Because they are always found in beds.

Tongue Twister

Repeat 3 times—out loud—as fast as you can
Seventy sailors sailed seven swift ships.

Question: How do you spell Mississippi with one eye?
Answer: Close one eye and spell it.

Question: When does rainfall make mistakes?
Answer: During a blunderstorm.

KNOCK, KNOCK.
Who's there?
Gillette.
Gillette who?
Gillette the cat out?

Question: What is always coming but never arrives?
Answer: Tomorrow.

Claude: What happens when 500 people rush to get accommodations in a hotel that only has 400 rooms?
Candice: Beats me.
Claude: They race for space.

---

*For the value of
wisdom is far above rubies;
nothing can be compared with it.*
Proverbs 8:11

A Note for You! _____

_____

_____

_____

_____

_____

Question: What did one volcano say to the other volcano?
Answer: I lava you so much.

Question: What you call a smoking mathematician?
Answer: A puff adder.

Tongue Twister

Repeat 3 times—out loud—as fast as you can
Sixty-six sickly chicks

Question: How does a clown fan himself?
Answer: He holds his hand still and waves his face in front of it.

69

KNOCK, KNOCK.
Who's there?
Atom.
Atom who?
Atom N. Eve.

Question: What do you call a person who's crazy about chocolate?
Answer: A cocoa-nut.

Cornelius: If Old Mother Hubbard gave a frankfurter to her dog, what kind of world would this be?
Claudia: I can't guess.
Cornelius: A dog-eat-dog world.

Wisdom and good judgment live together,
for wisdom knows where to discover
knowledge and understanding.
Proverbs 8:12

A Note for You! _____

_____

_____

_____

_____

Question: How slow was the man?
Answer: He was so slow that they had to show him how the wastebasket worked.

Question: Where is the capital of the United States?
Answer: All over the world.

Tongue Twister
Repeat 3 times—out loud—as fast as you can
Goofy gophers gobble goodies gladly.

Question: Why was Cleopatra so hard to get along with?
Answer: She was the queen of denial.

KNOCK, KNOCK.
Who's there?
Attack.
Attack who?
Attack is sharp if you sit on it.

Question: What is the right kind of lumber for castles in the air?
Answer: Sunbeams.

Conrad: Where does one see the handwriting on the wall?
Camilla: You tell me.
Conrad: In a phone booth.

If anyone respects and fears God, he will hate evil.
For wisdom hates pride, arrogance, corruption,
and deceit of every kind.
Proverbs 8:13

A Note for You! _____

_____

_____

_____

_____

_____

Question: What is red, has tusks, and hates to be touched?
Answer: An elephant with a sunburn.

Question: What was the elephant doing in the road?
Answer: About 3 miles an hour.

Tongue Twister

Repeat 3 times—out loud—as fast as you can:
Silly Lilly slithered slightly slyly, slowly slinging silver slivers.

Question: What happens to a man who claws his way over the desert on Christmas day?
Answer: He gets sandy claws.

KNOCK, KNOCK.
Who's there?
Augusta.
Augusta who?
Augusta wind blew my hat off.

———

Question: What do you call a sunburn on your stomach?
Answer: A pot roast.

———

Question: Why did Humpty Dumpty fall off the wall?
Answer: To make the nursery rhyme go right.

———

Question: How do you become a coroner?
Answer: You have to take a stiff examination.

———

Teach a wise man, and he will be the wiser;
teach a good man, and he will learn more.
Proverbs 9:9

A Note for You! _____

_____

_____

_____

_____

Question: What happened when your little girl got married?
Answer: I didn't lose a daughter, I gained a son. He moved in with us.

Tongue Twister

Repeat 3 times—out loud—as fast as you can:
Cows graze in groves on grass which grows in groves.

Question: Where would you send a man to get a big appetite?
Answer: To Hungary.

KNOCK, KNOCK.
Who's there?
Avenue.
Avenue who?
Avenue knocked on this door before?

Question: Do you know how long tall cows should be milked?
Answer: Of course. The same as short ones.

Clifford: What do you call a crate full of ducks?
Cordelia: Who knows?
Clifford: A box of quackers.

For the reverence and fear of God
are basic to all wisdom. Knowing God
results in every other kind of understanding.
Proverbs 9:10

A Note for You! _____

_____

_____

_____

_____

Question: Where does a sheep get its haircut?
Answer: At the baa-baa shop.

Tongue Twister

Repeat 3 times—out loud—as fast as you can
Chilly Charlie Schilling surely chopped shallots and chive.

Question: What's the quickest way to collect on your life insurance?
Answer: Tell a hippo that his mother wears combat boots.

KNOCK, KNOCK.
Who's there?
Avon.
Avon who?
The Avon lady.
Your doorbell isn't working.

Question: What do you say when you meet a two-headed monster?
Answer: Hello, hello.

Question: Who is the oldest whistler in the world?
Answer: The wind.

Ill-gotten gain
brings no lasting happiness;
right living does.
Proverbs 10:2

A Note for You! _____

_____

_____

_____

_____

Question: What do you call a newborn beetle?
Answer: A baby buggy.

Question: What keeps the moon from falling?
Answer: Its beams, of course.

Tongue Twister

Repeat 3 times—out loud—as fast as you can:
Six slippery, sliding snakes.

Question: What two letters got kicked out of the alphabet for being rotten?
Answer: D—K.

KNOCK, KNOCK.
Who's there?
Ax.
Ax who?
Ax your mother if you can come out and play.

Question: How did the rocket lose its job?
Answer: He was fired.

Question: What did the judge say when the skunk came in the courtroom?
Answer: Odor in the court.

Christopher: What is the definition of a Chinese harbor?
Clara: That's a mystery.
Christopher: A junkyard.

Lazy men are soon poor; hard workers get rich.
Proverbs 10:4

A Note for You! _____

_____

_____

_____

_____

Question: What did the chewing gum say to the shoe?
Answer: I'm stuck on you.

Tongue Twister
Repeat 3 times—out loud—as fast as you can:
How many clans can a cloner clone if a
cloner can clone clans?

KNOCK, KNOCK.
Who's there?
Bay.
Bay who?
Bay be face, you've got the cutest
little baby face!

Question: What did one tailpipe say to the other tailpipe?
Answer: I'm exhausted.

Jeff: What floats on the water as light as a feather, yet a thousand men can't lift it?
Noel: I'm blank.
Jeff: A bubble.

A wise youth makes hay while the sun shines,
but what a shame to see a lad who sleeps
away his hour of opportunity.
Proverbs 10:5

A Note for You! _____

_____

_____

_____

_____

Question: Why did the teacher give the student an F minus?
Answer: She said he not only didn't learn anything new, but he probably forgot most of the stuff he learned last year as well.

Tongue Twister
Repeat 3 times—out loud—as fast as you can
"Gee whiz, show biz," said Ms. Diz Fizz.

Question: What is purple and crazy?
Answer: A grape nut.

KNOCK, KNOCK.

Who's there?
Be.
Be who?
Be down to get you in a taxi, honey.

————

Question: Why did the boy take a hammer to bed with him?
Answer: He wanted to hit the sack.

————

Barnaby: What comes in handy when you have a flat tire?
Basil: I don't have the foggiest.
Barnaby: Despair.

————

Question: What is the value of the moon?
Answer: Four quarters.

————

Hatred stirs old quarrels, but love overlooks insults.
Proverbs 10:12

A Note for You! _____

_____

_____

_____

_____

Question: What do you get if you cross a steer with a tadpole?
Answer: A bull frog.

Tongue Twister

Repeat 3 times—out loud—as fast as you can:
Eight angry alligators ate eight awful apricots.

Question: What happens when a flock of geese lands in a volcano?
Answer: They cook their own gooses.

KNOCK, KNOCK.

Who's there?
Beckon.
Beckon who?
Beckon goes well with eggs.

Question: Why are telephone rates so high in Iran?
Answer: Because everyone speaks Persian-to-Persian.

Christy: Did you hear about the poet who got arrested for writing too fast?
Cornelia: No, what about him?
Christy: The judge took away his poetic license.

A wise man holds his tongue.
Only a fool blurts out everything he knows;
that only leads to sorrow and trouble.
Proverbs 10:14

A Note for You! _____

_____

_____

_____

_____

Question: What happens when you are submerged in water?
Answer: The telephone rings.

Question: What did one elevator say to the other elevator?
Answer: I think I'm coming down with something.

Tongue Twister

Repeat 3 times—out loud—as fast as you can:
Pet's pa, Pete, poked to the pea patch to pick a peck of peas
for the poor pink pig in the pine hole pig pen.

Question: What do you get when you cross an elephant with a computer?
Answer: A 5,000 pound know-it-all.

KNOCK, KNOCK.

Who's there?

Ben.

Ben who?

Ben down and tie my shoes, please.

Question: Why did the whale cross the road?
Answer: To get to the other tide.

Mary: Harry, let's go jogging together.
Harry: Why?
Mary: My doctor told me I could lose weight by working out with a dumbbell.

Don't talk so much.
You keep putting your foot in your mouth.
Be sensible and turn off the flow!
Proverbs 10:19

A Note for You! _____

_____

_____

_____

_____

Question: What is the best thing to put in a pie?
Answer: Your teeth.

Question: What becomes of most love triangles?
Answer: They turn into wreck-tangles.

Tongue Twister

Repeat 3 times—out loud—as fast as you can:
Sure the ship's shipshape, sir.

Question: What's the longest word in the dictionary?
Answer: Smiles. There's a mile between the first and last letter.

89

KNOCK, KNOCK.

Who's there?
Bob.
Who?
Bob, Bob black sheep,
have you any wool?

Question: What do you call a veterinarian with laryngitis?
Answer: A hoarse doctor

Lisa: How many psychiatrists does it take to screw in a light bulb?
Lola: You've got me.
Lisa: Only one. But the light bulb really has to want to change.

When a good man speaks, he is worth listening to,
but the words of fools are a dime a dozen.
Proverbs 10:20

A Note for You! _____

_____

_____

_____

_____

_____

Question: What is a turtle?
Answer: A reptile who lives in a mobile home.

Question: What kind of fish is the most stupid?
Answer: A simple salmon?

Tongue Twister
Repeat 3 times—out loud—as fast as you can:
Good blood, bad blood.

Question: Why did the traffic light turn red?
Answer: If you had to change in front of all those people, you'd turn red too.

KNOCK, KNOCK.

Who's there?

Boop.

Boop who?

Boop-boopie

doo.

Question: Who can stay single even after he marries many women?

Answer: A minister.

Henrietta: What is the best way to grow fat?

Ruby: My mind is a blank.

Henrietta: Raise pigs.

---

*The Lord's blessing
is our greatest wealth.*
Proverbs 10:22

A Note for You! _____

_____

_____

_____

_____

_____

Question: What did the sea say to the shore?
Answer: Nothing. It just waved.

Tongue Twister

Repeat 3 times—out loud—as fast as you can:
This shop stocks short socks with stripes and spots.

Question: What does the plumber say to his wife when she talks too much?
Answer: Pipe down.

Question: Who serves a four-year term of office, signs documents, and rattles?
Answer: The President of the United Snakes.

KNOCK, KNOCK.
Who's there?
Butch, Jimmy, and Joe.
Butch, Jimmy, and Joe who?
Butch your arms around me,
Jimmy a hug, or I'll Joe home.

———

Question: What word do most people like best?
Answer: The last.

———

Hector: What has antlers and eats cheese?
Harlow: That's a mystery.
Hector: Mickey Moose.

———

*The Lord hates cheating
and delights in honesty.*
Proverbs 11:1

A Note for You! _____

_____

_____

_____

_____

Question: Why did you charge me $10 and all you did was paint my throat?
Answer: What did you expect for $10—wallpaper?

Tongue Twister
Repeat 3 times—out loud—as fast as you can:
Timmy Tomkins tripped Tommy Timkins.

Question: How often do big ocean liners sink?
Answer: Only once.

KNOCK, KNOCK.
Who's there?
Butcher.
Butcher who?
Butcher feet on the floor.

Question: What do you call a crazy man who lives at the mouth of the Amazon?
Answer: A Brazil nut.

Pam: What headlines do women like least?
Melba: I have no idea.
Pam: Wrinkles.

A good man is guided by his honesty;
the evil man is destroyed
by his dishonesty.
Proverbs 11:3

A Note for You! _____

_____

_____

_____

_____

Question: What do they call the device that keeps flies in the house?
Answer: A window screen.

Question: What well-known animal drives an automobile?
Answer: The road hog.

Tongue Twister
Repeat 3 times—out loud—as fast as you can:
Yellow yo-yo's you yo-yo's use.

Question: What kind of sea creature is like an expression of disbelief?
Answer: Abalone.

KNOCK, KNOCK.
Who's there?
Butter.
Butter who?
Butter be home before
midnight.

Question: Name a carpenter's tool you can spell forward and backward the same way.
Answer: A level.

Question: When is it bad luck to have a black cat follow you?
Answer: When you are a mouse.

To quarrel with a neighbor is foolish;
a man with good sense
holds his tongue.
Proverbs 11:12

A Note for You! _____

_____

_____

_____

_____

_____

Question: How do you make an elephant float?
Answer: Put him with two scoops of ice cream in a glass of soda.

———

Question: How does a dentist examine a crocodile's teeth?
Answer: Very carefully.

———

Tongue Twister
Repeat 3 times—out loud—as fast as you can:
There is a pleasant peasant present.

———

Question: How do amoebas break up with their girlfriends?
Answer: They split.

KNOCK, KNOCK.
Who's there?
Butternut.
Butternut who?
Butternut try to pick
up a skunk.

Kevin: When do the numbers 10 plus 7 equal 13?
Cory: Search me.
Kevin: When you add wrong.

Question: What do they call it when a Cub Scout washes his hands?
Answer: Erosion.

A gossip goes around spreading rumors,
while a trustworthy man tries to quiet them.
Proverbs 11:13

A Note for You! _____

_____

_____

_____

_____

Question: What's the best way to paint a rabbit?
Answer: With hare spray.

Tongue Twister

Repeat 3 times—out loud—as fast as you can:
Theda thought thick thickets thinned thoroughly.

Question: What two opposites mean the same thing?
Answer: Half-full and half-empty.

KNOCK, KNOCK.

Who's there?

Bwana.

Bwana who?

Bwana hold your hand.

Question: What is big and green and eats rocks?

Answer: A big green rock-eater.

Question: Why does a person who is sick lose his sense of touch?

Answer: Because he doesn't feel well.

---

*Your own soul is nourished
when you are kind; it
is destroyed when
you are cruel.*
Proverbs 11:17

A Note for You! _____

_____

_____

_____

_____

Question: Why is the stork associated with birth?
Answer: Because we all come into this world stork naked.

Tongue Twister

Repeat 3 times—out loud—as fast as you can:
The wild wolf roams the wintry wastes.

Question: What do they call a textbook wired for sound?
Answer: A professor.

Question: Where do you find tigers?
Answer: It depends on where you leave them.

KNOCK, KNOCK.
Who's there?
Caesar.
Caesar who?
Caesar jolly good
fellow.

———

Question: What happened when the dog visited the flea circus?
Answer: He stole the show.

———

Jon-Mark: What animal doesn't play fair?
Jonas: Beats me.
Jon-Mark: The cheetah.

———

The Lord hates the stubborn
but delights in those
who are good.
Proverbs 11:20

A Note for You! _____

_____

_____

_____

_____

_____

Question: Why are writers the strangest creatures in the world?
Answer: Because their tales come out of their heads.

Question: How long is a Chinaman?
Answer: Of course. How Long *is* his name.

Tongue Twister

Repeat 3 times—out loud—as fast as you can:
Busby Bee boldly buzzed by Benji Bear.

Question: Why is a wig like a lie?
Answer: Because it's a falsehood.

KNOCK, KNOCK.
Who's there?
Cameron.
Cameron who?
Cameron film are what you need
to take pictures.

Question: Where does a pig go to pawn his watch.
Answer: He goes to the ham hock shop.

Customer: Does the manager know you've knocked over this whole pile of canned tomatoes?
Stock boy: I think so. He's underneath.

If you search for good,
you will find God's favor;
if you search for evil,
you will find his curse.
Proverbs 11:27

A Note for You! _____

_____

_____

_____

_____

Question: What goes ha-ha-ha-plop?
Answer: Someone who laughs his head off.

Tongue Twister

Repeat 3 times—out loud—as fast as you can:
A real red rooster roosts in the rain.

Question: What do we need armies for?
Answer: To keep our handies on.

KNOCK, KNOCK.

Who's there?

A herd.

A herd who?

A herd you were home, so I came over.

Question: How do you keep an elephant from going through the eye of a needle?
Answer: Tie a knot in its tail.

Teacher: If you took three apples from a basket that contain 13 apples, how many apples would you have?
Student: If you took three apples, you'd have three apples.

Godly men are growing a tree
that bears life-giving fruit, and all
who win souls are wise.
Proverbs 11:30

A Note for You! _____

_____

_____

_____

_____

Question: What do you call someone who steals pigs?
Answer: A hamburglar.

Tongue Twister

Repeat 3 times—out loud—as fast as you can:
Tuesday is stew day. Stew day is Tuesday.

Question: What kind of clothes do Supreme Court judges wear?
Answer: Lawsuits.

Question: What is another name for a cracked pot?
Answer: A psycho-ceramic.

Question: What steps should you take if a tiger charges you?
Answer: Long ones.

KNOCK, KNOCK.
Who's there?
Candy.
Candy who?
Candy bell ring?
I'm tired of knocking.

Question: Which is larger, Mr. Larger, or Mr. Larger's baby?
Answer: The baby is a little Larger.

Speaker: A horrible thing has happened. I just lost my wallet with $500 in it. I'll give $50 to anyone who will return it.
Voice from the rear: I'll give $100.

To learn,
you must want to be taught.
To refuse reproof is stupid.
Proverbs 12:1

A Note for You! _____

_____

_____

_____

_____

Question: Why did the farmer put the cow on the scale?
Answer: He wanted to see how much the milky weighed.

Tongue Twister
Repeat 3 times—out loud—as fast as you can:
"Jump, Judy, jump," Ginny Jenkins jabbered joyfully.

Question: Why should a man never tell his secrets in a cornfield?
Answer: Because there are too many ears out there, and they might be shocked.

KNOCK, KNOCK.
Who's there?
Dewey.
Dewey who?
Dewey have to listen to
all this knocking?

Question: What do you get if you cross a skeleton with a great detective?
Answer: Sherlock Bones.

Question: What kind of robbery may not be dangerous?
Answer: A safe robbery.

Wickedness never
brings real success; only the godly
have that.
Proverbs 12:3

A Note for You! _____

_____

_____

_____

_____

Owen: The doctor opened the window wide. He said to me, "Stick your tongue out the window."
Clayton: What for?
Owen: He said, "I'm mad at one of my neighbors."

Question: What is the Lone Ranger's first name?
Answer: The.

Tongue Twister
Repeat 3 times—out loud—as fast as you can:
Let little Nellie run a little.

Question: What was Snow White's brother's name?
Answer: Egg white . . . (get the yolk?)

KNOCK, KNOCK.
Who's there?
Canoe.
Canoe who?
Canoe help me with my homework?

Question: Why does electricity shock people?
Answer: Because it doesn't know how to conduct itself.

Question: Which key is the hardest to turn?
Answer: A donkey.

Boss: You are recommending Jack for a raise? I can't believe it—he is the laziest worker!
Foreman: Yes, but his snoring keeps the other workers awake!

A good man's mind is filled with honest thoughts;
an evil man's mind is crammed with lies.
Proverbs 12:5

A Note for You! _____

_____

_____

_____

_____

Question: How bad is the food in your cafeteria?
Answer: It's so bad that they caught a mouse trying to phone out for pizza.

Question: What did one bowl of pudding say to the other bowl of pudding?
Answer: You're pudding me on.

Tongue Twister
Repeat 3 times—out loud—as fast as you can:
"Hi, Harry Healy," hollered Holly Heartily.

KNOCK, KNOCK.
Who's there?
Cantaloupe.
Cantaloupe who?
Cantaloupe without a ladder.

Question: What did one horse say to the other?
Answer: I can't remember your mane but your pace is familiar.

Employer: And you say you've been fired from 10 different jobs?
Worker: Well, my father always said, "Never be a quitter!"

Everyone admires
a man with good sense,
but a man with a warped mind
is despised.
Proverbs 12:8

A Note for You! _____

_____

_____

_____

_____

Question: What is the new award that Italy is sponsoring for making the best pizza?
Answer: The Nobel Pizza Prize.

Question: What will stay hot longest in the refrigerator?
Answer: Red pepper.

Tongue Twister

Repeat 3 times—out loud—as fast as you can:
The sailor's tailor thoroughly failed furling.

Question: Which is the best side of the bed to sleep on?
Answer: The top side.

KNOCK, KNOCK.
Who's there?
Carfare.
Carfare who?
Carfare a cookie or a piece of pie?

Question: What did one stuck-up person say to another?
Answer: Nothing.

Winifred: Why did the Three Little Pigs decide to leave home?
Myrtle: That's a mystery.
Winifred: They thought their father was an awful boar.

---

*It is better to get
your hands dirty—and eat,
than to be too proud to work—and starve.*
Proverbs 12:9

A Note for You! _____

_____

_____

_____

_____

Question: Why did the man lose his shoes?
Answer: He put them on the wrong feet and then couldn't remember whose feet he put them on.

Tongue Twister

Repeat 3 times—out loud—as fast as you can:
Fat Matt the cat pats the rat in the hat.

Question: What is the difference between the rising sun and the setting sun?
Answer: All the difference in the world.

KNOCK, KNOCK.
Who's there?
Carmen.
Carmen who?
Carmen get it if you're hungry.

Question: Who rides a dog and was a Confederate general during the Civil War?
Answer: Robert E. Flea.

Looney Linda: Don't you ever peel a banana before eating it?
Looney Larry: No. I already know what's inside.

A good man is concerned
for the welfare of his animals,
but even the kindness of
godless men is cruel.
Proverbs 12:10

A Note for You! _____

_____

_____

_____

_____

Question: What do you call a nut that never remembers?
Answer: A forget-me-nut.

Tongue Twister

Repeat 3 times—out loud—as fast as you can:
If one doctor doctors another, does the doctor who doctors the
doctor, doctor the same way the doctor he is doctoring doctors?
Or does he doctor the doctor the way the
doctor who doctors doctors?

KNOCK, KNOCK.
Who's there?
Turner.
Turner who?
Turner handle and
please let me in.

Question: How far is it from one end of the earth to the other?
Answer: A day's journey. The sun does it in a day.

Willard: What is the difference between a hungry person and
a greedy person?
Wally: I give up.
Willard: One longs to eat and the other eats too long.

Hard work means prosperity;
only a fool idles away his time.
Proverbs 12:11

A Note for You! _____

_____

_____

_____

_____

_____

Question: If a gardener has a green thumb, who has a purple thumb?

Answer: A nearsighted plumber.

Tongue Twister

Repeat 3 times—out loud—as fast as you can:
I never smelled a smelt that smelled as bad
as that smelt smelled.

KNOCK, KNOCK.
Who's there?
Diesel.
Diesel who?
Diesel be your last chance
to open the door.

———

Question: What's the most popular gardening magazine?
Answer: Weeder's Digest.

———

Harry: Why would you expect a fisherman to be more honest than a shepherd?
Kerry: Who knows?
Harry: Because a fisherman lives by hook and a shepherd lives by crook.

———

Crooks are jealous of each other's loot,
while good men long to help each other.
Proverbs 12:12

A Note for You! _____

_____

_____

_____

_____

Question: What is green and pecks on trees?
Answer: Woody Wood Pickle.

Question: What is the difference between a cat and a match?
Answer: One lights on its feet and the other lights on its head.

Tongue Twister

Repeat 3 times—out loud—as fast as you can:
Fran fans Fred frantically.

Question: What do they call someone who can stick to a diet?
Answer: A good loser.

KNOCK, KNOCK.
Who's there?
Della.
Della who?
Della Katessen.

Question: When is a black dog not a black dog?
Answer: When he is a Greyhound.

Ned: When is an elevator not an elevator?
Jed: I have no idea.
Ned: When it's going down.

Lies will get
any man into trouble,
but honesty is its
own defense.
Proverbs 12:13

A Note for You! _____

_____

_____

_____

_____

Question: Why did the umpire throw the chicken out of the game?

Answer: He suspected fowl play.

Tongue Twister

Repeat 3 times—out loud—as fast as you can:
Six selfish shellfish.

KNOCK, KNOCK.
Who's there?
Distress.
Distress who?
Distress hardly covers
my knees.

Question: If your dog was eating your book, what would you do?
Answer: I would take the words right out of his mouth.

Tom: How can you tell a Jersey cow from any other cow?
Jerry: You've got me.
Tom: By its license plate.

Telling the truth
gives a man great satisfaction,
and hard work returns many blessings to him.
Proverbs 12:14

A Note for You! _____

_____

_____

_____

_____

_____

Question: What is flat at the bottom, pointed at the top, and has ears?
Answer: A mountaineer.

Question: What will change a pear into a pearl?
Answer: The letter L.

Tongue Twister
Repeat 3 times—out loud—as fast as you can:
Dirty Danny Dig didn't dig dirt,
did he?

Question: What happens when a chimpanzee twists his ankle?
Answer: He gets a monkey wrench.

KNOCK, KNOCK.
Who's there?
Disjoint.
Disjoint who?
Disjoint is closed.

Question: What do you call a carpenter who lends tools to his neighbor?
Answer: A saw loser.

Bill: If joy is the opposite of sorrow, what is the opposite of woe?
Jill: I have no clue.
Bill: Giddyup.

The character of even a child
can be known by the way he acts—whether
what he does is pure and right.
Proverbs 20:11

A Note for You! _____

_____

_____

_____

_____

Question: What do you get if you light a duck's tail?
Answer: A firequacker.

Question: What do you do for someone who splits his sides with laughter?
Answer: Have him run as fast as he can 'til he gets a stitch in his side.

Tongue Twister

Repeat 3 times—out loud—as fast as you can:
Lisbeth lisps lengthy lessons.

Question: What's the biggest laundry problem giraffes have?
Answer: Ring around the collar.

KNOCK, KNOCK.
Who's there?
Dishes.
Dishes who?
Dishes me. Who ish you?

Question: If all the money in the world were divided equally among the people, how much would each person get?
Answer: An equal amount.

Clyde: Who rides in a sleigh, gives Christmas presents, and has many faults?
Carlotta: I can't guess.
Clyde: Santa Flaws.

---

*If you have good
eyesight and good hearing,
thank God who gave them to you.*
Proverbs 20:12

A Note for You! _____

_____

_____

_____

_____

Question: What is the best way to keep a skunk from smelling?

Answer: Hold his nose.

Tongue Twister

Repeat 3 times—out loud—as fast as you can:
Fast Freddie Frog fries fat flying fish.

Question: What is so brittle that it can be broken by just naming it?

Answer: Silence.

Question: With what two animals do you always go to bed?

Answer: Two calves.

KNOCK, KNOCK.

Who's there?

Pecan.

Pecan who?

Pecan someone your own size!

Question: What do you call a crate full of ducks?
Answer: A box of quackers.

Clyde: Why should men avoid the letter A?
Carlotta: I don't know.
Clyde: Because it makes men mean.

If you love sleep,
you will end in poverty.
Stay awake, work hard, and there
will be plenty to eat!
Proverbs 20:13

A Note for You! _____

_____

_____

_____

_____

Question: What is the difference between a chocolate chip cookie and an elephant?
Answer: You can't dunk an elephant in your milk.

Question: What two things can you never eat for breakfast?
Answer: Lunch and dinner.

Tongue Twister

Repeat 3 times—out loud—as fast as you can:
Lucky Louie Lion likes licking lemon lollipops.

Question: Why is a sleeping baby like a hijacking?
Answer: Because it's a kid napping.

KNOCK, KNOCK.

Who's there?
Distress.
Distress who?
Distress is pretty
don't you think?

Question: What two numbers together make 13?
Answer: One and three.

Clyde: Why does Uncle Sam wear red, white, and blue suspenders?
Carlotta: I don't know.
Clyde: To hold up his pants.

---

*Good sense is
far more valuable than gold
or precious jewels.*
Proverbs 20:15

A Note for You! _____

_____

_____

_____

_____

Question: What is orange, runs on batteries, and costs six million dollars?
Answer: The Bionic Carrot.

Question: If an apple a day keeps the doctor away, what does an onion do?
Answer: It keeps EVERYBODY away.

Tongue Twister

Repeat 3 times—out loud—as fast as you can:
Literally literary literature.

Question: What is gross stupidity?
Answer: One hundred and forty-four goofy people.

KNOCK, KNOCK.
Who's there?
Divan.
Divan who?
Divan the pool–I'm drowning.

Question: What floats on water as light as a feather, yet a thousand men can't lift it?
Answer: A bubble.

Clyde: What does a worm do in a cornfield?
Carlotta: I have no idea.
Clyde: It goes in one ear and out the other.

---

*Don't tell your secrets
to a gossip unless you want them
broadcast to the world.*
Proverbs 20:19

A Note for You! _____

_____

_____

_____

_____

Question: How many members of your Loony family does it take to screw in a light bulb?
Answer: What's a light bulb?

Question: Where does a two-ton gorilla sit when he goes to the movies?
Answer: Anywhere he wants to!

Tongue Twister

Repeat 3 times—out loud—as fast as you can:
Sister Sue's silly song is softly sweet.

KNOCK, KNOCK.
Who's there?
Radio.
Radio who?
Radio not, here I come!

Question: What do Alexander the Great and Smoky the Bear have in common?
Answer: They both have the same middle name.

Clyde: What animal is satisfied with the least nourishment?
Claire: Beats me.
Clyde: Moths. They eat nothing but holes.

Don't repay evil for evil.
Wait for the Lord to
handle the matter.
Proverbs 20:22

A Note for You! _____

_____

_____

_____

_____

_____

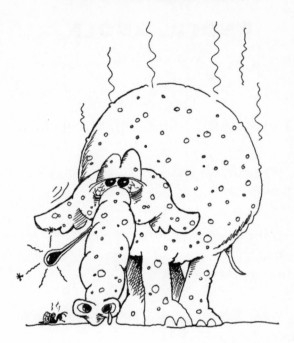

Question: What has spots, weighs four tons, and loves peanuts?
Answer: An elephant with the measles.

Question: Name two people who were never wrong?
Answer: Wilbur and Orville Wright.

Tongue Twister

Repeat 3 times—out loud—as fast as you can:
Nine nimble noblemen nibble nuts.

Question: What is found in the center of America and Australia?
Answer: The letter R.

KNOCK, KNOCK.
Who's there?
Doris.
Doris who?
Doris closed—that's why I knocked.

Question: What kind of jokes does a scholar make?
Answer: Wisecracks.

Question: If the man you work for weighs 2000 pounds, what do you call him?
Answer: Boston. (Boss ton)

Question: What do they call a man who gets paid for pinching people in the wrong places?
Answer: A policeman.

The Lord loathes all cheating and dishonesty.
Proverbs 20:23

A Note for You! _____

_____

_____

_____

_____

Question: Why did the man put a camera on his fishook?
Answer: To take pictures of the fish that got away.

Question: What do they call a fellow who introduces his best girl to his best friend?
Answer: Very trusting!

Tongue Twister

Repeat 3 times—out loud—as fast as you can:
How many bagels could a beagle bake
if a beagle could bake bagels?

KNOCK, KNOCK.

Who's there?

Dozen.

Dozen who?

Dozen anybody want to let me in?

Question: What do they call a dollar with all the taxes taken out?
Answer: A nickel.

Clyde: What do you call a carrot who insults a farmer?
Carlotta: I give up.
Clyde: A fresh vegetable.

Since the Lord is directing our steps,
why try to understand everything
that happens along the way?
Proverbs 20:24

A Note for You! _____

_____

_____

_____

_____

Question: What do you call a frightened skin diver?
Answer: Chicken of the sea.

Question: Why did Uncle Oscar name both of his sons Ed?
Answer: Because he had heard that two Eds are better than one.

Tongue Twister

Repeat 3 times—out loud—as fast as you can:
Windy weather makes Wendy Worm wiggle wildly.

Question: Who was the first man to make a monkey out of himself?
Answer: Darwin.

KNOCK, KNOCK.
Who's there?
Duke.
Duke who?
Duke the halls with
boughs of holly.

———

Question: When is it alright to lie?
Answer: When you are in bed.

———

Clyde: What has one eye, one horn, and flies?
Carlotta: I have no idea.
Clyde: A half-blind rhinoceros in an airplane.

———

*A man's conscience
is the Lord's searchlight
exposing his hidden motives.*
Proverbs 20:27

A Note for You! _____

_____

_____

_____

_____

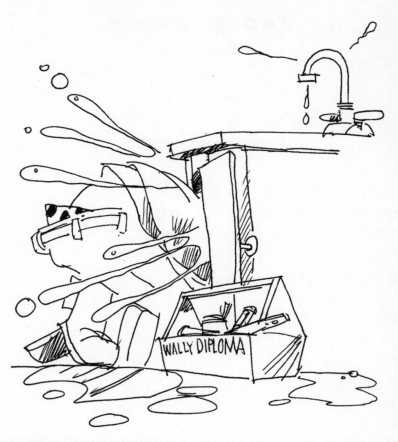

Question: What is a diploma?
Answer: Da man who fixa da pipes when dey leak.

Question: What is the definition of a Chinese harbor?
Answer: A junk yard.

Tongue Twister
Repeat 3 times—out loud—as fast as you can:
Blame the big bleak black book!

147

KNOCK, KNOCK.
Who's there?
Duncan.
Duncan who?
Duncan doughnuts
in your milk makes
'em soft.

———

Question: Which animal keeps the best time?
Answer: A watchdog.

———

Question: What do you get when you cross a hummingbird with a bell?
Answer: A humdinger.

———

Punishment that hurts
chases evil from the heart.
Proverbs 20:30

A Note for You! _____

_____

_____

_____

_____

Question: When is a basketball player like a baby?
Answer: When he dribbles.

***

Question: What's the best thing to do if you're going to be beheaded?
Answer: Stay calm and try not to lose your head.

***

Tongue Twister

Repeat 3 times—out loud—as fast as you can:
Tuesday Timmy told two tall tales to Tommy Tucker.

***

Question: What is it called when a man marries the boss' daughter.
Answer: Fire insurance.

KNOCK, KNOCK.
Who's there?
Dwayne.
Dwayne who?
Dwayne the bathtub,
I'm drowning

Question: Why do giraffes find it difficult to apologize?
Answer: It takes them a long time to swallow their pride.

Clyde: What does Jack's giant do when he plays football?
Carlotta: My mind is a blank.
Clyde: He fee-fi-fo-fumbles.

---

*We can justify
our every deed, but God
looks at our motives.*
Proverbs 21:2

A Note for You! _____

_____

_____

_____

_____

_____

Question: Why did the prizefighter like his new job?
Answer: He got to punch the time clock.

Question: When does a farmer have the best chance to see his pigs?
Answer: When he has a sty on his eye.

Tongue Twister
Repeat 3 times—out loud—as fast as you can:
"Hark! An ark lark!" barked Bart.

Question: What's wrong with overeating?
Answer: It makes you thick to your stomach.

KNOCK, KNOCK.

Who's there?
Dynamite.
Dynamite who?
Dynamite play with us
if we behave.

Question: What grows larger the more you take away?
Answer: A hole.

Clyde: What man slept in his clothes for 100 years?
Carlotta: That's a mystery.
Clyde: Rip Van Wrinkled.

---

*Dishonest gain
will never last, so why
take the risk?*
Proverbs 21:6

A Note for You! _____

_____

_____

_____

_____

Question: Do ears of corn get dandruff?
Answer: Sure. Haven't you ever heard of corn flakes?

Question: Why are spiders good baseball players?
Answer: Because they know how to catch flies .

Tongue Twister
Repeat 3 times—out loud—as fast as you can:
She says she shall sew a sheet.

Question: Which bird can lift the heaviest weight?
Answer: The crane.

KNOCK, KNOCK.
Who's there?
Eclipse.
Eclipse who?
Eclipse my hair in the
barber shop.

Question: What do hippopotamuses have that no other animals have?
Answer: Baby hippopotamuses.

Clyde: What do whales do when they feel sad?
Carlotta: I don't have the foggiest.
Clyde: Blubber.

A man is known by his actions.
An evil man lives an evil life;
a good man lives a godly life.
Proverbs 21:8

A Note for You! _____

_____

_____

_____

_____

_____

Question: What do you get if you hit a gopher with a golf ball?
Answer: A mole-in-one.

Question: What goes putt-putt-putt-putt?
Answer: An over-par golfer.

Tongue Twister

Repeat 3 times—out loud—as fast as you can:
A queer quick questioning quiz.

Question: Where is the best place to find books about trees?
Answer: A branch library.

KNOCK, KNOCK.
Who's there?
Edsall.
Edsall who?
Edsall there is—there
isn't anymore.

———

Question: What did the man do when he heard was going to die?
Answer: He went into the living room.

———

Clyde: What kind of soda can't you drink?
Carlotta: Don't ask me.
Clyde: Baking soda.

———

*The wise man saves for the future,
but the foolish man spends
whatever he gets.*
Proverbs 21:20

A Note for You! _____

_____

_____

_____

_____

Question: What room can no one enter?
Answer: A mushroom.

Question: What color is a hiccup?
Answer: Burple.

Tongue Twister

Repeat 3 times—out loud—as fast as you can:
A big black bug bit a big black bear.
Where is the big black bear the big black bug bit?

Question: What is the longest sentence in the world?
Answer: "Go to prison for life."

KNOCK, KNOCK.
Who's there?
Howie.
Howie who?
Fine thanks. Howie you?

Question: What is the last thing you take off before going to bed?
Answer: Your feet from the floor.

Clyde: What kinds of toys does a psychiatrist's child play with?
Carlotta: I'm in the dark.
Clyde: Mental blocks.

The man who tries to be good, loving,
and kind finds life, righteousness,
and honor.
Proverbs 21:21

A Note for You! _____

_____

_____

_____

_____

_____

Question: How do you make a hot dog stand?
Answer: Take away its chair.

Question: What did the mayonnaise say to the refrigerator?
Answer: "Shut the door, I'm dressing."

Tongue Twister

Repeat 3 times—out loud—as fast as you can:
Seth hoes Beth's rows.

Question: Where do fish go to get a degree?
Answer: To tuna-versities.

KNOCK, KNOCK.
Who's there?
Egypt.
Egypt who?
Egypt me when he
gave me change!

———

Question: What is full of holes and yet holds water?
Answer: A sponge.

———

Clyde: What two garden vegetables fight crime?
Carlotta: Search me.
Clyde: Beetman and Radish.

———

*Keep your mouth closed
and you'll stay out
of trouble.*
Proverbs 21:23

A Note for You! _____

_____

_____

_____

_____

_____

Question: What do you get if you drop Limburger cheese in the toaster?
Answer: You get out of the kitchen as fast as you can.

———

Question: What is another name for a smart duck?
Answer: A wise quacker.

———

Tongue Twister
Repeat 3 times—out loud—as fast as you can:
Miss Smith dismisseth us.

———

Question: Why did the chicken cross the road?
Answer: For fowl reasons.

161

KNOCK, KNOCK.

Who's there?
Eileen.
Eileen who?
Eileen on a
walking stick.

Question: What has a foot at each end and a foot in the middle?
Answer: A yardstick.

Clyde: Why did the rich lady buy a Ming vase?
Carlotta: I have no clue.
Clyde: To go with her Ming coat.

No one believes a liar,
but everyone respects the words
of an honest man.
Proverbs 21:23

A Note for You! _____

_____

_____

_____

_____

Question: How did you get burns on the both your ears?
Answer: The phone rang and I picked up the steam iron by mistake.
Question: But what about the other ear?
Answer: They called back.

Question: What is the center of gravity?
Answer: V.

Tongue Twister
Repeat 3 times—out loud—as fast as you can:
Ron Watts runs rat races.

KNOCK, KNOCK.
Who's there?
Eileen.
Eileen who?
Eileen over to tie my shoes.

———

Question: What did the Gingerbread Boy find on his bed?
Answer: A cookie sheet, of course!

———

Question: What is the best thing about tiny TV sets?
Answer: Tiny commercials.

———

Clyde: Why do elephants have ivory tusks?
Carlotta: I don't know.
Clyde: Iron tusks would rust.

———

Happy is the generous man,
the one who feeds the poor.
Proverbs 22:9

A Note for You! _____

_____

_____

_____

_____

Question: What did the fly say to the waiter?
Answer: There's a guy in my soup!

Question: Who was the world's greatest glutton?
Answer: A man who bolted a door, then threw up a window, and sat down and swallowed a whole story.

Tongue Twister

Repeat 3 times—out loud—as fast as you can:
Wee Willy whistles to wise Wilbur Whale.

KNOCK, KNOCK.

Who's there?

Elder.

Elder who?

Elder in my arms all evening.

Question: If you were dying and you only had fifty cents, what would you buy?

Answer: A pack of lifesavers.

Clyde: Why would a man in jail want to catch the measles?

Carlotta: I have no idea.

Clyde: So he could break out.

Keep away from angry,
short-tempered men,
lest you learn to be like them
and endanger your soul.
Proverbs 22:24

A Note for You! _____

_____

_____

_____

_____

Question: Which animal keeps the best time?
Answer: A watchdog.

Question: What happened to the duck that flew upside down?
Answer: It quacked up.

Tongue Twister

Repeat 3 times—out loud—as fast as you can:
Thin sticks, thick bricks.

Question: What kind of song do you sing in a car?
Answer: A cartoon.

KNOCK, KNOCK.
Who's there?
Elephants.
Elephants who?
Elephants Gerald,
the singer.

———

Question: If you got locked in a cemetery at night, how would you get out?
Answer: Use a skeleton key.

———

Clyde: What bone can't a dog eat?
Carlotta: Beats me.
Clyde: A trombone.

———

Telling lies about someone is as harmful
as hitting him with an axe, or wounding him with a sword,
or shooting him with a sharp arrow.
Proverbs 25:18

A Note for You! _____

_____

_____

_____

_____

Question: How do you communicate with a fish?
Answer: Drop it a line.

Question: What did Paul Revere say when he finished his famous ride?
Answer: Whoa!

Tongue Twister

Repeat 3 times—out loud—as fast as you can:
Monday morning mother made mincemeat pies.

Question: What is worse than raining cats and dogs?
Answer: Hailing taxis and buses.

KNOCK, KNOCK.

Who's there?

Ellison.

Ellison who?

Ellison the alphabet after K.

Question: To what question must you positively answer "Yes"?

Answer: What does Y-E-S spell?

Clyde: What do you get when you trip an elephant carrying a crate of oranges.

Carlotta: You tell me.

Clyde: Orange juice.

Yanking a dog's ears is no more foolish
than interfering in an argument that isn't
any of your business.
Proverbs 26:17

A Note for You! _____

_____

_____

_____

_____

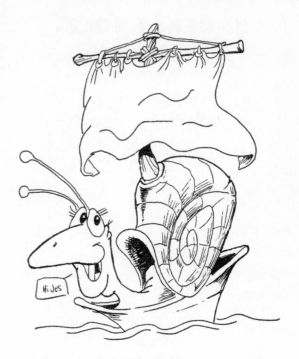

Question: What is the world's slowest ship?
Answer: A snailboat.

Question: What makes more noise than a cat howling at midnight?
Answer: Two cats howling at midnight.

Tongue Twister

Repeat 3 times—out loud—as fast as you can:
A bootblack blacks boots with a black blacking brush.

Question: How does a musician clean a dirty tuba?
Answer: With a tuba toothpaste, naturally!

KNOCK, KNOCK.
Who's there?
Emerson.
Emerson who?
Emerson big eyes you've
got, kiddo.

Question: What is the difference between an engineer and a teacher?
Answer: One minds the train, while the other trains the mind.

Question: Where do you find the finest basements?
Answer: On the best-cellar list.

Jealousy is more
dangerous and cruel
than anger.
Proverbs 27:4

A Note for You! _____

_____

_____

_____

_____

Question: What happens to illegally parked frogs?
Answer: They get toad away.

Question: What is worse than a centipede with corns?
Answer: A hippopotamus with chapped lips.

Tongue Twister
Repeat 3 times—out loud—as fast as you can:
Bob's job's to rob gobs of fobs.

Question: What does everybody give and few take?
Answer: Advice.

KNOCK, KNOCK.
Who's there?
Ether.
Ether who?
Ether bunny.

———

Question: Why was it that Mrs. Jones had given her neighbor a butter churn, and her neighbor gave her one back?
Answer: Because one good churn deserves another.

———

Clyde: What is another name for a cowboy?
Carlotta: Who knows?
Clyde: A bull.

———

*Hard work
brings prosperity;
playing around brings poverty.*
Proverbs 28:19

A Note for You! _____

_____

_____

_____

_____

Question: Why won't they let wacky people become paratroopers?
Answer: They can't count to ten.

Question: Why is an empty purse always the same?
Answer: Because there is never any change in it.

Tongue Twister
Repeat 3 times—out loud—as fast as you can:
Pure food for four pure mules.

KNOCK, KNOCK.
Who's there?
Hop.
Hop who?
Hop, hop away,
Ether bunny gone.

———•••———

Question: Why is it hard to talk with a goat around?
Answer: Because he always butts in.

———•••———

Clyde: What kind of bird eats the same worm eight times?
Carlotta: You've got me.
Clyde: A swallow with the hiccups.

———•••———

Fools start fights everywhere
while wise men try
to keep peace.
Proverbs 29:8

A Note for You! _____

_____

_____

_____

_____

Question: Why does a hen lay an egg?
Answer: Because she can't lay a brick.

Question: How do you mail a boat?
Answer: You ship it.

Tongue Twister

Repeat 3 times—out loud—as fast as you can:
Pretty pink pigs pile pea pods on paper plates.

KNOCK, KNOCK.
Who's there?
Cargo.
Cargo who?
Cargo beep and ran over
the Ether bunny.

———•••—

Question: What is deaf, dumb, and blind and always tells the truth?
Answer: A mirror.

———•••—

Clyde: What do you do if there's a kidnapping in Texas?
Carlotta: My mind is a blank.
Clyde: Wake him up.

———•••—

A rebel shouts in anger;
a wise man holds his temper in and cools it.
Proverbs 29:11

A Note for You! _____

_____

_____

_____

_____

Question: What do you get when a bird flies into a fan?
Answer: Shredded tweet.

Question: Why did the little boy go to sleep with birdseed in his shoes?
Answer: He wanted to feed his pigeon toes.

Tongue Twister
Repeat 3 times—out loud—as fast as you can:
Flesh of fresh flying fish.

Question: What do you call a dumb skeleton?
Answer: A bone head.

KNOCK, KNOCK.

Who's there?

Boo.

Boo who?

Don't cry—Ether bunny be
back next year!

Question: What is the surest way to double your money?
Answer: Fold it in half.

Clyde: What does Mickey Mouse's girlfriend wear?
Carlotta: That's a mystery.
Clyde: Minnie skirts.

There is more hope for a fool
than for a man of
quick temper.
Proverbs 29:20

A Note for You! _____

_____

_____

_____

_____